NOTES from THE EDITOR

Jessica L. Mosley

Here we are again for the June issue of the MizCEO Entreprenurial Magazine! To God be all the glory!

In this issue we focus on The Power of PERSEVERANCE! In business, that is something that you definitely have to have. The articles contained here within will show you how to keep going during your hardest, most difficult times in business.

Our double cover fearure stories are some pretty phenomenal women! Dr.Lisa Ward, Owner and Creator of the Hey Beautiful brand and Yolanda Jerry, Owner and Creator of YJEmpowers, are people that one definitely wants to be on the look out for in 2018!

Grab your favorite mug. Pour your favorite tea. And be sure get in a good, distraction free, quiet spot. Because this issue is sure to bring you motivation, inspiration, and information on how to persevere through during those difficult times in business.

Because He Lives,

Jessica L. Mosley

CONTRIBUTORS

CONTRIBUTING
-WRITERS-

PUBLISHER - J.MOSLEY PUBLISHING I DESIGN - CAMDEN LANECREATIVE AGENCY

DWAN BRYANT

SHANICK BARTELL

JACQUELINE MILLER

DELISA WILLIAMS

CHERYL PEAVY

AUDREY WOODLEY

LASHEERA LEE

SHIRLONDA TAYLOR

JOHNNEICE ARRIAGO

SANTISHA WALKER, RN

DR. LESLIE HODGE

DIAMOND

DR. DEENA BROWN

PRIYA WILLIAMS

WHAT'S INSIDE

TABLE OF CONTENTS

Page 4 ....Cover Story - Yolanda Jerry - Don't give up...P.U.SH.

Page 7 ....Sisters Creative Media

Page 8 ....Girl you can do it! LaSheera Lee

Page 10 ....The Unstoppable Tenacity Erica Stepteau by Cheryl Peavy

Page 13 ....The Wives by Delisa Williams

Page 17 ....Shinar

Page 18 ....Sherilyn Bennett - A Leap of Faith!

Page 19 ....Johane Filemon by Jacqueline Miller

Page 21 ....Joy Sinegar - Fearless by Shirlonda Taylor

Page 22 ....Lisa Lewis Ellis - A heart to serve

Page 24 ....Anita Hawkins by Dr. Leslie Hodge

Page 26 ....Chonté Nichol - From Pain to Purpose by Shanick Bartell

Page 30 ....All About Chelsea (Stalling) Whittington

Page 32 ....Jill And Jokima - The Literary Life

Page 34 ....Health and Wellness by Santisha Walker

Page 36 ....Lasalle Jackson by Dwan Bryant

Page 37 ....Necoya Tyson - Planning with Purpose

Hey Beautiful

To purchase visit www.lisawardinspires.com

LisaKaye

SIGNATURE COLLECTION

COVER STORY - YOLANDA JERRY

Don't Give Up...
P.U.S.H.

*"Like a moth to a flame
Burned by the fire
That's the way
My love is blind
Can't you see my desire
That's the way love goes"*
- Janet Jackson

Like a moth to a golden flame entrepreneurs flock to the "trep" lifestyle thinking it will be all glory and glamorous; realistically speaking entrepreneurship requires a complete transformation, a metamorphosis. **"Accept the Past, Focus on the now, Impact the Future!"** Yolanda Jerry.

Yolanda Jerry, author, activist, and amazing veteran entrepreneur has some authentic insight into how to PUSH through when life happens and you need to break free from the cocoons that limit the boundaries of your personal and professional success.

Yolanda Jerry served 20 years in the United States Air Force where she spent nine years as a Certified Sexual Assault Victim Advocate. Yolanda's transition into entrepreneurship has been full of self-discovery and just like the beautiful butterfly, a hallmark for her brand, Yolanda has transformed her skill-sets into a dynamic business that has global impact. It was enlightening to interview the incomparable Yolanda Jerry, CEO of YJ Empowerment Solutions, LLC who has a deeper conceptual definition of entrepreneurship.

COVER STORY - YOLANDA JERRY CONT'D

Dr. Deena: How Do you Define Entrepreneurship?
Yolanda: Entrepreneurship is a process. Being an entrepreneur is about designing something you have a vision and passion for. Your vision is something you want to see grow and manifest to impact others around the world as part of your legacy. Entrepreneurship is about planting seeds and touching peoples life which can be profitable but more importantly it should be memorable, it is about legacy building. *"Your Set Back Is A Set Up For A Major Come Back!"* - Yolanda Jerry

Dr. Deena: What was your motivation to actually SHIFT into entrepreneurship?
Yolanda: The motivation has always been there ...I wanted to embark on this journey after I left the military. My first logo that is interwoven into my current brand was S.A.V.E.D. It stands for Saved, Spiritual, Anointed, Valuable, Equipped, and Delivered. This speaks of who I am. However, what really PUSHed me was my Dad. When my dad fell ill in January 2015 from congestive heart failure I had to make a SHIFT. It put a temporary hold on my plans but it didn't stop me. My dad has always been and always will be my greatest motivation and inspiration. My dad told me *"Do not stop what you wanted to do before I got sick. I will be around."* My dad is always present. His legacy lives on in me and everything I do. The butterfly in my logo represents my dad. After two years my dad passed and now I am honoring his vision, mission, and goals for my life. I told my dad, "Daddy ....I am gonna do it." Guess what, I did!

"Sometimes God will put a Goliath in your life for you to find the David in you." - Dr. Deena C. Brown

Dr. Deena: In addition to the memory of your dad what helps you process and SHIFT to the next level?
Yolanda: The first thing I do every morning is pray and meditate. My dad and the word of God are the two things that keep me going. My dad had a powerful walk with God and he instilled the power of the word of God into my life. My dad broke down scripture so that I could always relate it to my life's journey. It is not about religion but more about relationship. It is about the people that you are trying to reach.

Dr. Deena: Not every caterpillar that starts the journey becomes a butterfly. What advice would you give to new entrepreneurial who are embarking on an entrepreneurial journey?
Yolanda: It will be a struggle in order for you to make progress. You have to put in the work. It will not happen overnight. The more you invest in yourself the more your vision will come to light. Do your background checks and spend the money required to achieve the results you desire. Ask questions and do not be afraid to start over. You don't have to do it alone ask for help
and advice and surround yourself with positive people that want to see you succeed. The biggest advice I could give is to "GET OVER YOURSELF."

Metamorphosis; a change of the form or nature of a thing or person into a completely different one, by natural or supernatural means.

Yolanda Jerry, CEO of YJ Empowerment Solutions, envisions a life after and free from violence, assault and depression. She is ready to empower victims/survivors by helping them lead from the inside as they experience their own personal metamorphosis to move from a traumatic experience to confidence in self.

CONT'D ON PAGE 25

SISTERS CREATIVE MEDIA: A LEAP OF FAITH

By LaSheera Lee

Letrise decided to step out on faith to launch her small business Sistah's Creative Media. Benefiting from her 17 years in Corporate America as Accounting Manager compliments her creative side with operational mindset of running a business. She holds a Masters degree in Financial Management and Bachelor's degree in Accounting

MIZCEO What drives you to pursue your Passion?
I am driven by my vision and dreams that ignites my passion to pursue my own business. The joy of being in control and building something that I believe in, love, and feel happiness that puts a huge smile on my face. The thought of know that I can leave something for my children and their children.

MIZCEO What are some obstacles you face in your perspective business?
All business face obstacles; however, one that is not uncommonly to women in business is being the "new kid on the block". Another obstacle would be learning to identify customers who are serious from those who are wasting your time.

MIZCEO Do you feel that being a woman has hindered your progress in this field?
No, I do not feel that being a woman has hindered my progress in this field. I say this because there are so many women in my field of media & entertainment who have successful run companies.

MIZCEO What are some business tips you can share with other women?
Business tips I want other women to have would be the following:
- Define your mission
- Make sure your vision is clear
- It' okay to Rebrand your business so that it will continue to grow
- Learn from your mistakes- they will make you stronger
- Don't be afraid to ask for help – you are not super woman.
- Learn to delegate tasks
- Invest in knowledge for you can never not know enough

MIZCEO What is next on your agenda?
For my media business Sistah's Creative Media, it is to branch out and partner with likeminded business women that will allow us to grow and reach more clients. For Sistah's Place it is to launch my the digital online magazine with Issuu Publications that will create more exposure for minority men and women in literary, film, theater, television, music, artist, activists, and small business. The long term goal for both business is to become global company.

La Sheera Lee is an award winning blogger, podcaster, moderator, and vision delegate. She loves to help people to see the beauty in their voices. You can catch her on podcast called Read You Later on Blog Talk Radio or iHeart Radio. Follow her on Twitter and Instagram @readyoulater

ENTREPRENEUR ARISE!

Girl you can do it!

By LaSheera Lee

Women, especially women of color are flooding the entrepreneurial field, at a record rate.

Women of color no longer feel that have to stay on the sidelines. Honey, women of color are showing up and showing out. That being said, often, when you are first in your circle to lay the blueprint, you don't have a guide to use. I am going to share some tips to get you on track.

Vision
God's vision and purpose for us are greater than we can imagine. In His word He states *"For I know the plans I have for you," declares the LORD, "plans to prosper you and not to harm you, plans to give you hope and a future." Jeremiah 22:11.* Are you thinking too small? Are you belittling your efforts to make others around you feel comfortable. Girl, I see you. I know you all too well. Being there, done that. If I can have a transparent moment, I still have to fight myself out that box. God has gifted you with talents. He has anointed you for certain task. Get! Out!. Of! Your! Way! You are called to greatness. Be great! Move with grace and humility but move.

Business Plan
"And the Lord answered me, and said, Write the vision, and make it plain upon tables, that he may run that readeth it." Habakkuk 2:2 Are you attempting to run a business by the seat of your pants? If so, you need to immediately formulate a business plan. Your business plan should not be generic. The plan should be specific to your needs. If you are looking for investors, the plan should be specific to that need. If you want a business loan, that plan should support that fact. The plan should be realistic and be able to function as an arm of your company. There are various templates on the Internet. However, getting information from your local Small Business Association can be very beneficial and vital to the success of your company. Often they have classes for free or nominal prices. It is also a good place to network with other companies and perhaps potential investors.

GIRL YOU CAN DO IT! CONT'D PAGE 12

THE UNSTOPPABLE TENACITY

Queen

ERICA STEPTEAU
By Cheryl Peavy

Who is Erica Stepteau?
Erica is a Growth & Sales Strategist a.k.a Queen Coach Erica who empowers women to master the art of selling so that they catapult their IMPACT, MONEY, and FREEDOM. Erica has been an online entrepreneur since 2012 and struggled for years to charge her worth because she was afraid people wouldn't be able to afford services, but she had a wakeup call when she was FLAT BROKE with 16 Clients and working 14-16hours day! She was charging only $100 for Health Coaching services (Weekly 60mins sessions, Weekly meal planning, Weekly fitness, and UNLIMITED email services. She was overworked and UNDERPAID. She was so frustrated because she had the same feelings of being a "slave" to her business as she did working a 9-5 job. In addition, She was investing MORE into her business than the monthly business income. Enough was enough! She muscled up the courage to triple those rates at that time and kept climbing the ladder to a level she could have never imagined!

The biggest lesson she have learned in these years is that the price you set on your programs/services communicates the confidence you have in your skills and your belief that you CAN solve your clients' problem! She also realized that she was blocking herself from the life she desired. Erica knew she desired TIME & FINANCIAL FREEDOM which required to earn $10, 000/month or more. However, she couldn't ever achieve that goal charging those tiny prices and working that many hours in a day.

Now she is on a mission to empower 1 million entrepreneurs to charge what they're worth and show them that they don't have to be sleazy, gimmicky, or overly assertive to create the abundance they desire in their biz with her GUARANTEED signature system. Heart-Center Entrepreneurs can authentically sell programs/services with EASE like a Queen Boss!

What is Unstoppable Tenacity?
Unstoppable Tenacity is a declaration to claim your inheritance and create the life you have always dreamed of. Most of the time it's our emotional baggage and gremlins preventing us from being "unstoppable".

ERICA STEPTEAU - ALL HAILE THE QUEEN CONT'D

Unstoppable Tenacity empowers women of all ages and any socioeconomic status to be tenacious on their journey by pushing beyond thoughts of scarcity, past failures, potential obstacles, or lack of resources.

What is your definition of Perseverance?
Perseverance (in my opinion) is pushing beyond the comfort zone, expanding yourself until your rubber band of limitations snaps, turn challenges into opportunities, and examine the conditions of your heart in order to rise up and claim your UNSTOPPABLE TENACITY!

In walking in your purpose you have been faced with a lot of challenges what were some of them? And how did you overcome them? Is there steps that you can share in persevering in obtaining ones goals?
My Book *Unstoppable Tenacity* is compiled of 42 bite-sized chapters sharing 42 D.I.Ps (Distractions, Interruptions, Pitfalls) I have experienced in my life. I have been through A LOT in my lifetime so far: Childhood Molestation, Financial woes, Bankruptcy, Lack of Direction in purpose, Job loss, Military Deployments, Family Discord, but the most challenging and mind-boggling circumstance I am STILL working on every day of my life is my 15 year infertility journey. My husband and I have had 5 natural miscarriages and invested thousands of dollars in various treatments with no results. It's a mindset battle that most do not understand nor even try to understand. Everyone is very quick to say, "oh honey, it will happen on God's timing" or "Its probably best the way life is for you guys since you get to be free" or "Go adopt a baby and I bet you will get pregnant". We have heard it ALL in this 15-year journey; no one will have the words to soothe the pain, doubt, and fears associated with this frustration. As an ambitious woman it taps into my ego because I have this crazy drive to MAKE IT HAPPEN WHEN I WANT IT TO HAPPEN. However, this journey requires pure submission, trust, and faith. That is why my husband and I cherish EVERY moment together via traveling and extracurricular activities. We have been together for 20 years and enjoy each other's company like we've started dating a year ago. We ensure we live life to the FULLEST, NO MATTER WHAT.

I created a quote to encourage myself and others on how to overcome challenges which you feel like they are out of your control:

"When life gives you lemons...make lemonade, lemon meringue pie, lemon cupcakes, and lemon rum iced drinks". -Erica Stepteau

In a nutshell, this quote states: make the best of the situation and keep it moving! Every circumstance we face is a "state of mind".

You quit your 9-5 to become a full-time entrepreneur and walk by faith, share what did you do? I recall you ended up rebranding yourself. What made you do this?
In November 2017 I was able to resign my position at a world-renowned medical institution because I strategically 5 Times my Salary and gained clarity on why I developed the Unstoppable Tenacity movement in the first place. I naturally attracted entrepreneurs who were struggling with business profits in their brand. I would coach women on a daily basis: empowering them to charge what they're worth, providing tips on positioning themselves as the expert, and closing sales with their prospects. It was only natural to make it public and known to everyone that Business Growth & Sales was a natural gift I possessed and a HUGE need for my clients. That is when Tenacious Queen Academy was

ERICA STEPTEAU - ALL HAILE THE QUEEN CONT'D

birthed to the world!

What advice can you give women who are pursuing their purpose and becoming an entrepreneur?
I call my tribe Tenacious Queens because we are stubborn about our goals, the money we earn, and the lifestyle we desire for ourselves and family. The stubbornness becomes our drive and daily motivation to never give up. The main advice I have for an aspiring entrepreneur is to first connect with self by making sure you are aligned with your business mission, be super clear about the problem you desire to solve for your client, and consistently position yourself as the authoritative figure in your industry. These are the ingredients to Command REPEAT clients!

What is next for Erica?
On 04/29 the Tenacious Queen Brand is launching a $7K in 7 Days Challenge. The challenge is to provide HANDS-ON training to position their brand for $1K days with EASE and FLOW! We will be examining a 7-Step Sales Process developed through my trials, obstacles, and lessons learned in my 6 year journey as an Online Entrepreneur.

How can women connect with you?
Tenacious Queens Unite FB Group https://m.facebook.com/groups/115408493798754

GIRL YOU CAN DO IT! CONT'D FROM PAGE 8

Read
It is okay to read books for pleasure but you also need to read books for business growth. Find experts in your field that have written books that will help you take your business to the next level. Also, read books about marketing and business models tips. If you are short on cash, go to your local library and checkout books. Knowledge is power.

La Sheera Lee is an award winning blogger, podcaster, moderator, and vision delegate. She loves to help people to see the beauty in their voices. You can catch her on podcast called Read You Later on Blog Talk Radio or iHeart Radio. Follow her on Twitter and Instagram @readyoulater

THE WIVES | PRESERVERANCE

From 4 to 3...And then there were 2!:
A STORY OF PURPOSE, PRAYER, AND PERSISTENCE TO KEEP GOING AND FULFILL GOD'S VISION

By Delisa Williams

The Wives, Authors and Entrepreneurs DeLisa New Williams and Kristen R. Harris have been on a mission committed to saving billions of marriages, one wife at a time. Together these ladies work hard and pray even harder while educating women on the success in marriage through social media, social events, workshops, and seminars like the most recent one hosted at The Black Women's Expo Chicago. With recent achievements such as newly published books, The Wives Wednesday radio show, and many booked speaking engagements; it wasn't always the glitz and glam you see now.

In the beginning, it's always beautiful. You have this great idea and you just know once you present it to the world, they'll fall in love with it too. But next comes the hard work, sleepless nights, hours of praying, and most importantly the financial investment or lack thereof. When The Wives began it started off all that and more, seriously. The idea of 4 women each using their gifts and talents to create a platform for wives and wives-in-waiting, sounded wonderful...euphoric even. The vision was executed with months of planning and hour long meetings. Events were scheduled and radio interviews were in full effect. Even Rolling Out did an article about the birth of the talk show called The Wives.

Within months after debuting the brand to the world with a huge event that sold out within weeks, one of The Wives' member resigned and decided to pursue other endeavors, but still remained close with the ladies. After a year of branding themselves with just 3 members, other opportunities arouse and fell into the lap of another wife leaving the trio to a duo.

With any business, vision, or great idea being built from the ground up you'll experience some hiccups and setbacks along the way. How do you persevere through it all when in the beginning everything seemed so good like a dream finally becoming reality? **How do you continue to push past every obstacle coming your way and continue on with the vision you believe God has given you?**

THE WIVES - PRESERVERANCE CON'TD

They just want to show everyone the good, but not the bad nor the ugly. Well, we are very transparent when it comes to sharing our truth. Our Facebook Group, The Wives Hive can attest to that because we're always sharing some story or testimony about our marriage in hopes that it will save another couple. So when two of the members left, we didn't allow it to affect us from moving forward with the mission God had called us to. See a lot of times entrepreneurs want to focus on what went wrong and just quit, instead of figuring out how to make it right and persevere. We even joked about it many times and said, "Hey, if Destiny's Child can do it and come back from it, so can we!". Being entrepreneurs ourselves (Kristen owns a couture treat company called, "Pizzazzed Plus" and DeLisa owns a custom apparel company called "The Hem of HIS Garment, Inc.") we've learned how to not cry over spilled milk, talk to God, remember your mission, trust the dream, and move on despite what
curveballs the enemy tries to throw your way.

What are some of your challenges today?
One of the major challenges that we are currently helping the women that we serve truly understand that they need what we have to offer. Day to day, we witness so many struggling marriages and we are equipped with the tools and resources that can help them. However, many either do not know that they need the assistance, and in some cases, they do not want the help. It can be extremely challenging and frustrating having a cure but the diseased won't acknowledge what you have to offer.

Wow, so what would you like to tell the readers who may be experiencing the same thing and want to quit? Any tips?
Our advice to anyone who is experiencing a similar challenge would be to remember why you are on this journey in the first place. Holding on to your why can keep you encouraged to keep pushing even when it seems like your information is falling on deaf ears. This strategy has worked well in overcoming our challenges because we have held on tightly to our mission. "The Wives are on a mission to save marriages one WIFE at a time." If our message reaches one woman and helps to transform her marriage, we have done well! Also, remember every bump in the road isn't set to throw you off course. It might just be there to show that you can handle whatever obstacles may come your way and walk out being victorious and successful through it all. It's all apart of God's plan!

What's new for The Wives?
We have some exciting things on the horizon for both

THE WIVES - PRESERVERANCE CON'TD

the wife and the wife-in-waiting. This year, we have also decided to pull our husbands in to start building up other men. It is our desire to truly transform the Black family, starting with the nucleus of the home -- the husband and the wife. Additionally, we will be launching a midwest tour with the purpose of empowering wives and women across the country.

Photo Credit: Billy Montgomery Photography and He Shoots Lyfe Event Photography You can find more about The Wives at www.thewivestalk.com and on Facebook, Twitter, and Instagram at @TheWivesTalk. On Wednesday nights at 7:30PM EST, catch them on www.wllfradio.com to hear exciting interviews, interesting topics, and more.

SHINAR - CONFIDENCE PERSONIFIDE

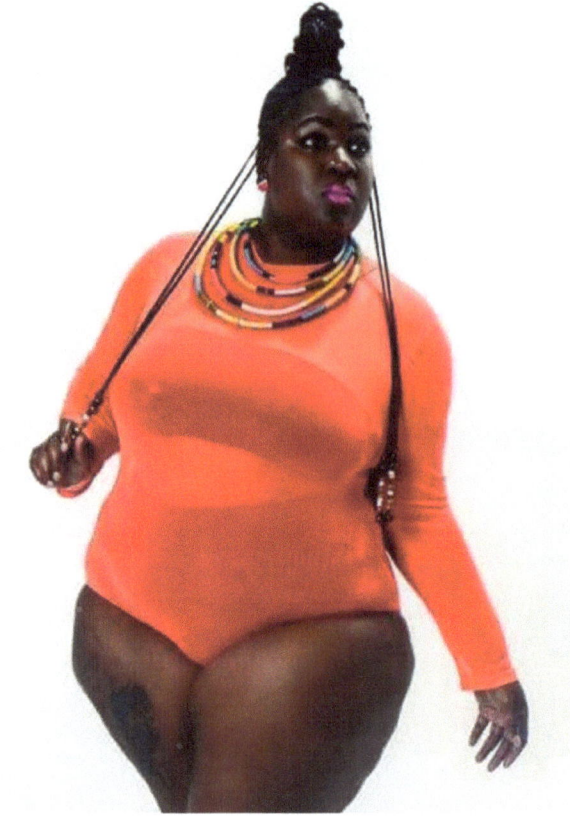

MizCEO: Introduce yourself and profession to our readers:
Shinar: My name is Shinar S. Martin. I am 29 yrs old Single and No kids. I am very Optimistic about My future. My Profession is that I am Model, Confidence Coach, and An Advocate for Body Positivity.

MizCEO: What inspired you to pursue this area of interest?
Shinar: I got inspired to Model about 5 yrs ago when I saw Plus Size Models we're on the rise. What Pursed me and inspired me to be a Confidence Coach was the Gift that God gave me. Which is to simply seek after Women Hearts to heal them Emotionally and Mentally with Expressing and Showing them how to love thy self.

MizCEO: What advice would you share with those interested in a similar pursuit?
Shinar: My advice to those in similar pursuit such as myself, is to follow your heart and that will lead you to your Great Success in Your Business

MizCEO: Discuss a professional challenge and how you overcame it:
Shinar: Professional Challenge i have came across would be, is that i had to learn how to let go and walk away. Learn when Your Assignment is done.

MizCEO: What is next for your brand/business in 2018?
Shinar: New for My Brand/Business 2018, Nov. i will be hosting My Sec. Annual Body Positivity Seminar and I will also be launching My T-Shirt Line!! I will also be conducting 4- 6 week Confidence Training Classes!!

MizCEO: How can readers connect with you online and through social media
Shinar: Everyone can reach and connect with me on FB/ **Shinar S. Martin IG/ Shinar_themodel** or my email **MartinShinar@gmail.com**

SHERILYN BENNETT - A LEAP OF FAITH

MizCEO: How did you get into your business?
Sherilyn: I launched Camden Lane Creative Agency after being laid off from my job of 6 years. I have not looked back. That pink slip changed my life.

MizCEO: How do you handle stress in your business?
Sherilyn: Entrepreneurship is indeed stressful. Sometimes you can feel like everything falls on your shoulder and most of the time it does. I am a graphic designer/branding expert so most of my time is spent at the computer. When I am stressed I step away from the office and take a walk or call a friend for lunch. A change of environment helps me deal with stress.

MizCEO: What is your biggest hurdle you've overcome since becoming a business owner?
Sherilyn: One of the biggest hurdles I have overcome thus far is not being intimidated by the financial side of owning a business. I overcame that by understanding that I may not know everything but I don't have to there are professional people that I can hire to take care of the things I am not versed in.

MizCEO: What is the biggest achievement you've accomplished with your business?
Sherilyn: One of the biggest achievements for my creative agency is having wonderful clients who are Grammy and Dove nominated as well as my partnership with TBN (Trinity Broadcasting Network) to brand their new authors for the Trilogy Publishing House. We are also proud of our brand for women in business, LEAP! Birth. Brand + Build. We have amazing things ahead for the LEAP Brand.

MizCEO: In your opinion, what is the key to success?
Sherilyn: Success to me means having the ability to live my life doing what I love. Having my gifts and talents provide financial stability for me. In addition, leaving a legacy for other women and equipping them to walk out their own entrepreneurial journey.

MizCEO: The best business tip you can give a prospective person who is looking to merge into your field?
Sherilyn: Be patient, always do business with integrity, and never leave your faith out of your business decisions.

MizCEO: What is a quote/mantra that motivates you?
Sherilyn: You were born with everything you need to be the woman you will be. - Sherilyn Bennett

MizCEO: What advice would you give your younger self about growing up as a woman in this world?
Sherilyn: Trust your instinct and stand, even if you have to stand alone.

MizCEO: If you were the first woman president, what would be your first order of business?
Sherilyn: My first order of business would be to pass legislation to give women equal pay and recognition in the workforce and the marketplace and put prayer back in schools.

MizCEO: What was your last google search?
Sherilyn: I searched for Sarah Jakes Roberts website.

Sherilyn Bennett is an accomplished and sought-after national speaker. She is an award-winning designer, branding expert, and CEO of Camden Lane Creative Agency. Connect with her on facebook: Sherilyn Michelle Bennett, Camden Lane Creative Agency. Instagram: Sherilyn Bennett, Camden Lane Creative Agency. www.sherilyncreative.com

HEALTH AND WELLNESS

Johane Filemon
MS, RDN, CLT

By Jacqueline Miller

REGISTERED DIETITIAN NUTRITIONIST | OWNER OF WONDERFULLY NUTRITIOUS SOLUTIONS, LLC
PREVIOUSLY FEATURED IN ESSENCE MAGAZINE

How long have you been in the business of health & wellness?
I have been in private practice and operating my own business since 2014, but I've been in the nutrition field for 10+ years.

Why did you pick this particular field to do business in and what makes you and your business different from other similar businesses?
It's the craziest thing! Before college, I had never heard of a Dietitian or knew that the field of nutrition was one in which I could earn a degree. I went to college with the goal of going on to medical school in mind. I ended up choosing the route of Exercise Science -Pre-Med because I loved being active and I thought it was the perfect path to lead me to my goal of becoming a doctor. I discovered the field of nutrition because nutrition courses were a part of the requirements for my degree.

Being of Afro-Ancestry is rare in the field of nutrition. Most dietitians are of European descent. So, most who are looking to work with a dietitian, potential clients or otherwise, are likely to naturally gravitate towards those who look like them (i.e. European descent), even if not done out of malice. I grew up in a family where both my parents were culinary- trained, and subsequently I developed a love for food! My family is from Haiti so it was not uncommon for my dad to go to the backyard and select from the array of tea leaves that were growing so that he could create a remedy to relieve whatever was ailing us. I learned at an early age that food had healing properties. Identifying a field that incorporated my passion for food and my love for medicine was one of the best things that could have happened. It was a no-brainer that this was the field for me.

CONT'D ON PAGE 20

HEALTH AND WELLNESS - CONT'D

Why might someone possibly consider your success to be a fluke, a miracle, etc. because of circumstances that could have easily derailed you and your dream?

If someone were ever to tell me that my success was a result of luck I would have to show them just how hard I have worked and the obstacles that I had to overcome to get me to where I am today. God had plans for me from the start, and my success to date is definitely no fluke. My family immigrated to the United States from Haiti in 1989 and we found ourselves starting our lives all over from scratch. The careers, education, and socioeconomic status my parents acquired in Haiti, meant nothing when we got to the U.S. My parents had to begin to build their lives from the ground up and as a result, my upbringing was modest at best. However, because going to college was not an option, it was necessary; we found a way to secure finances needed for my educational opportunities, which led me to my current career.

What has been the GREATEST challenge (nearly made you want to give up) that you have faced since starting in this business and how you have overcome it?

The amount of student loans I had to take out to finance my education has been a major hindrance.
Money that could have been spent on my business and marketing must be spent on paying back my student loans. As a first-generation Haitian-American, my family did not have the financial capabilities to support my business at startup. I've had to fund my practice myself from the very beginning and both of
these factors have greatly affected my ability to grow my practice.

The second greatest challenge I've had thus far with starting my business was deciding whether I would be able to be a good mom to my boys and run a successful business. Feelings of guilt, along with thoughts of what I could potentially miss in my kids' lives while trying to build my practice, held me back for a while. With my husband's continued support, however, I realized that if I planned my schedule properly and managed my time effectively, I could make it happen. I also realized that the hard work that I would be faced with in the beginning phases of my business startup would slow down eventually. The long hours would not be forever and embracing this as reality helped to motivate me to proceed.

What would you say are the most significant obstacles to women maintaining and focusing on good health and how does your business provide a resolution?

Women are such caretakers by nature. We are consumed with taking care of others, our families, parents, siblings children, etc., that we forget to take care of ourselves. Years of neglect and stress can lead to weight gain and even disease. One of the programs that I offer in my practice is "My Mom Bod Retake". This program was designed to help mothers take back control of their bodies and their wellness so that they can live a healthy lifestyle= for themselves and their families.

What three health & wellness words of wisdom or tips do you have for women in 2018?

1. Take care of your wellness 1st before you take care of anyone else's!
2. Trust your gut, literally! Food can help and hurt us. Make sure that you are making wise food selections.
3. Don't be so hard on yourself. No one leads a perfect life.

In additions, a quote that I have used often in the last couple of years and that I believe in is as follows:
"Let food be thy medicine and medicine be thy food. " My interpretation of this is not to say that Western medicine should never be used because it does have its usefulness. It's to say that foods, including herbs, are very powerful and can be used to heal the body. It's my belief that "traditional" medicinal remedies should not always be the first ones to be considered.

For more information about Johane -
IG: @wonderfullynutritious
Facebook: Wonderfully Nutritious By Johane.

Jacqueline Miller is an international bestselling author, speaker, and certified life coach. Expert in empowering high-achieving women to excel in their lives, by providing strategies and resources to obtain clarity and techniques to successfully manage their careers, family obligations, relationships, finances, time management, and self-care. Stay connected with Jacqueline Miller by following her on social media. Facebook, Instagram and Twitter @mogulmomdujour as well as on LinkedIn: thejacquelinemiller

JOY SINEGAR - FEARLESS

By Shirlonda Taylor

Who Is Joy Sinegar?
I am a daughter, wife and mother who has a passion for helping people realize their financial dreams. I currently reside in the Chicagoland area but originally from Joliet.

Tell me a little about your education and experience (roles) you have had in Corporate America.
I obtained my degree from Louis University majoring in Computer Information Systems. Shortly thereafter during the time the Real Estate market was booming, I decided to jump in and got my license to sell real estate and from there became a Mortgage Loan Originator and Credit Coach. It was through the selling of Real Estate I found my true passion. Finance and Financial Literacy. Many borrowers were looking to purchase homes but I found people were not being properly educated when it came to the lending piece. That was 15 yrs ago and I have never looked backed! I'm currently a CRA (Community Reinvestment Act) for one of the top 10 banks it the country. Joy has won many awards and has been recognized on a national level for her lending abilities and the work she does in the communities in which she serves.

Why do you think it is important for Women of color to work in leadership roles and decision making capacities?
I think it is significant because not only does it inspire other women of color to achieve similar roles; it allows companies to receive a more in depth insight to the needs of consumers who are woman of color. The needs of this group can be ignored simply by lack of representation. We have so much to bring to the table. Women of Color are uniquely gifted and have the ability to look at the world's ill's and bring transformation that can be life changing. We have proven time after time our ability to make the impossible…..POSSIBLE.

What are some financial tips you would recommend for those who are looking to purchase a home this year?
• Open a saving Account
  (do not tie account to debit card)
• Commit to making regular payments each pay period
• Set reasonable goals
• Review your credit report for accuracy, dispute and payoff negative items

JOY SINEGAR - FEARLESS CONT'D

- Be sure to pay monthly bills ON TIME with NO 30 day lates
- Do not close account you have had for a long period of time with good pay history (this will cause a decrease in your credit score)

What advice would you give to someone who is just starting in the industry?
Don't do it! Just kidding! It is important, in my opinion, that anyone new to this industry must treat this endeavor like a work in progress. It's never perfect and you must be prepared for detours and uturns. You can fail and be successful at the same time. Surround yourself with people who know the industry and are more than just a "good lender". Yet in the end, bring your passion, drive & determination and the rewards will always be greater than any obstacle.

Joy Sinegar is a licensed Loan Originator and Credit Coach. Credit Warriors-Joy Sinegar Credit Coaching (Facebook group) visit her website https://mortgageapply.usbank.com/#/signup?referrerId=joy.sinegar%40usbank.com

LISA LEWIS ELLIS - A HEART TO SERVE

MizCEO: Who is Lisa at her core?
Lisa: At my core I am a woman that loves God and family! Putting my faith in action to serve God via serving my family and others is important to me.

MizCEO: Why are you so passionate about helping others live their best life?
Lisa: I'm living my best life and I want that for everyone else. You know how people say misery loves company? Well, having joy wants everyone to win and have good success! I believe that there are more than enough blessings, abundance, increase, peace, prosperity, success, etc. to go around. No competition because my blessings are in my lane and your blessings are in your lane.

MizCEO: Tell us about your businesses?
Lisa: I am in the business of teaching how to achieve prosperity and personal success by releasing self-limiting belief systems. I teach via four core service areas

Here's a brief rundown of my core services:
- **Coaching** – I will coach you in living the authentic, outside-the-box life you want! We will work together to release your self-limiting beliefs. Prosperity and personal success are within your reach.
- **Training** – Your hands are full juggling day-to-day life, and you don't have time for a group or individual coaching. However, in the wee hours of the morning, you can check emails and do some reading. Self-paced, virtual training will fit the bill to your liberation.
- **Speaking** – You said you weren't going to tell anybody, but deep down you know your community needs some "Lisa in their lives." And I'm here to give the people what they need. Book me to speak at your next empowerment event so your audience can experience a transformation like never before.
- **Spiritual Strategy** – God, is available 24/7. However, every now and again, you would like to have someone pray for you or touch base as an accountability partner. I'm available as a sidebar for prayer and spiritual strategizing as you align your soul for the good success you're working toward.

CONT'D ON PAGE 29

THE MizCEO
ENTREPRENEURIAL BRAND

What we offer:

Book/Magazine Publishing

Public Relations Services

Radio

Life/Business Coaching Services

ANITA HAWKINS - VICTORY IN THE STORM

No Explanation Needed

By Dr. Leslie Hodge

There's an old saying that a picture is worth a thousand words. If this is true, then a smile is worth a million. Nothing says hello like a smile - it is the best form of nonverbal communication. And what really speaks volumes, even in the midst of silence, is service with a smile.

Anita Hawkins' life speaks loud and clear of her dedication and commitment to serving others. From being a contractor, franchise owner, model, mentor, philanthropist, author, salon owner for 20 years, wife and mother, it is only fitting that she been dubbed a Lifestyle Expert Extraordinaire.

No stranger to hurt, pain, or obstacles, Anita can easily identify with people from all walks of life. A survivor of domestic violence, molestation, rape, and becoming a teen mom, she has not let any of those circumstances keep her from serving people. When Anita speaks, she speaks with the intention to help someone else. It is never about receiving sympathy it is always about giving hope. Understanding transparency is necessary for transformation, Anita always knew she had a story to tell. Bound by fear, she struggled within herself on how to share her story.

In 2011, fear and uncertainty met destiny. Anita received and accepted the assignment on her life to write a book that would change the lives of millions of women (and men). Giving herself 5 years to become an author, Anita completed her first literary work in 3 years. Writing her first book - *The Storm After the Storm*, was very therapeutic. It allowed Anita to freely and boldly share her story and be released from the limitations she had placed on herself, and the expectations she had placed on other people.

As discussed in her book The Storm After the Storm, it has not always been easy to smile. Fighting to find one reason to smile, Anita took what happened to her in her childhood and used it to develop her into the multifaceted powerhouse she is today.

Anita, a force to be reckoned with, takes what gifts she has been blessed with and creates solutions for the disparities she sees in communities. The reality of families not having access to the Prosper, Texas school districts or convenient healthy food options, were met with solutions when Anita began her journey of building her dream home. Met with countless challenges from the initial builder, Anita took matters into her own hands, obtained her contractor's license and founded Trokar Builders, LLC. Trokar Builders, LLC would not only complete the construction of her dream home, but purchase the only land zoned for starter homes in Propser, Texas. On this land, a subdivision full of starter homes were built, enabling families to have access to the elementary and middle schools in the highly acclaimed, award-winning school district. Trokar Builders, LLC, birthed from an unpleasant experience,

COVER STORY - YOLANDA JERRY CONT'D

Metamorphosis requires Leadhers to Don't Give Up …P.U.S.H™:

P-Persevere through the trials and tribulations to share your testimony.

U-Uncover your authentic truth; remember your why it will give you clarity on the how.

S- Shift according to your Divine narrative; You are who God says you are not who naysayers believe you should be.

H- Honor the journey; there is a burden in every blessing. The lessons are part of the growth process.

Achieving your goals is hardly ever an easy journey. If it were easy, we'd all already be there.

One of the keys to success is, without a doubt, perseverance. With improved perseverance you'll have that extra push from within to try, try again. have that extra push from within to try, try again.

Connect with Yolanda: www.IAMyolandajerry.com
facebook.com/yjempowers
Instagram @yj_empowerment_solutions

Dr. Deena C. Brown, The Chief LeadHer Officer, is a best-selling author, speaker, and certified John Maxwell Transformational Leadership Coach. Dr. Brown is the founder of The LeadherShift Movement™ for professional women who are ready to Shift to I CAN, I WILL, I DID by embracing the power of I AM. Instagram @Lead_Her_Shift FB: @LeadhershiftAcademy

ANITA HAWKINS - NO EXPLANATION NEEDED CONT'D

> "Don't Be Afraid of Reinventing You"

> I don't have expectations, but I do have requirements.

Trokar Builders, LLC, birthed from an unpleasant experience, not only changed the trajectory of Anita's life but would impact the community and generations to come.

Becoming ill and being diagnosed with Thalassemia – a genetic rare blood disorder, Anita was given two treatment options - to have blood transfusion or a blood marrow transplant. Not willing to settle for either, Anita opted to incorporate lifestyle changes in her daily routine. Faced with no convenient healthy restaurant options, Anita took her desire to own a restaurant and purchased the master franchise for Fresh Healthy Café for the Dallas-Fort Worth area. Not only did Fresh Healthy Café serve fresh healthy food, but also a fresh healthy serving of information and education, while providing a place for learning, meeting and keeping the community connected.

While Anita has never met a stranger, she also has not forgotten the importance of serving. Launching the Find One Reason To Smile campaign provides people with an opportunity to learn how to serve and how to put a smile on someone else's face. The latest campaign efforts include partnering with dentists and giving women real smiles with a full set of teeth - who have had their teeth knocked out by the aggressor or received drugs that caused deterioration while involved in sex trafficking.

Anita's commitment to be a voice for the voiceless enables her to serve selflessly with a smile. Some may not understand Anita's commitment to being a servant. But, when someone serves to help others become the best version of themselves…there is no explanation needed.

FROM PAIN TO PROMISE

By: Shanick Bartell

Social Media can paint a pretty picture at times. The pictures are painted with colors and hues of happiness, success, prosperity, and joy. If you didn't know better you would think you were the only one in the world facing challenges, setbacks, disappointments, and failures.

The fact is, it really isn't anyone's business what hardships and trials you're going through. However, lives can be changed when we step out from behind the beautiful posts and personal accolades and share our true stories. Stories that celebrate where we are now, but never forgetting the process that got us here. While we share the good, we recognize that the bad had to take place to get us there. Growing rarely ever takes place without growing pains. Sometimes humiliation yields humility, and sometimes humility is needed to walk into our destiny. Many people are out there stuck where we were, and because we persevered through the pain, we have the know how to help others do the same.

When I think of my topic perseverance I think of a young woman named Chonte' Nichol. At first glance, her tall, fashionable, striking appearance captivates you. Then you are completely drawn in when she shares her story of crawling through pain to walk into her promise. Who would've thought the journey to the promise all started with the click of a mouse on a social media site. Walk with me as we are inspired by her story.

Me: Nichol, how did this all start for you?
Chonte': (After letting out a vibrant laugh) It all started with a hashtag.

Me: Explain.
Chonte': Let me start at the beginning. I was going through a divorce. I was married with four children and let's just say, it ended. This wasn't a part of my life's plan and extremely painful as anyone could imagine. I was embarrassed, angry, mad, disappointed, and became bitter. For a year, I slept on my couch and didn't want to do anything. To release how I was feeling, I turned to social media. I shared my truth at that time and posted about my hurt, my pain, and other's part in it. It all changed when I was awakened in the middle of the night. God directed me to the

CHONTE' NICHOL - FROM PAIN TO PROMISE CONT'D

Social Media can paint a pretty picture at times. The pictures are painted with colors and hues of happiness, success, prosperity, and joy. If you didn't know better you would think you were the only one in the world facing challenges, setbacks, disappointments, and failures.

The fact is, it really isn't anyone's business what hardships and trials you're going through. However, lives can be changed when we step out from behind the beautiful posts and personal accolades and share our true stories. Stories that celebrate where we are now, but never forgetting the process that got us here. While we share the good, we recognize that the bad had to take place to get us there. Growing rarely ever takes place without growing pains. Sometimes humiliation yields humility, and sometimes humility is needed to walk into our destiny. Many people are out there stuck where we were, and because we persevered through the pain, we have the know how to help others do the same.

When I think of my topic perseverance I think of a young woman named Chonte' Nichol. At first glance, her tall, fashionable, striking appearance captivates you. Then you are completely drawn in when she shares her story of crawling through pain to walk into her promise. Who would've thought the journey to the promise all started with the click of a mouse on a social media site. Walk with me as we are inspired by her story.

Me: Nichol, how did this all start for you?
Chonte': (After letting out a vibrant laugh) It all started with a hashtag.

Me: Explain.
Chonte': Let me start at the beginning. I was going through a divorce. I was married with four children and let's just say, it ended. This wasn't a part of my life's plan and extremely painful as anyone could imagine. I was embarrassed, angry, mad, disappointed, and became bitter. For a year, I slept on my couch and didn't want to do anything. To release how I was feeling, I turned to social media. I shared my truth at that time and posted about my hurt, my pain, and other's part in it. It all changed when I was awakened in the middle of the night. God directed me to the scripture Isaiah 40:31 NIV version which states "but those who hope in the Lord will renew their strength, they will soar on wings like eagles; they will run and not grow weary, they will walk and not be faint. That yielded the hashtag, #WatchMeSoar. It started as a comeback. Oh, you think I'm gonna fail, well Watch Me Soar. Then God spoke to me telling me that I had to heal. I had to stop talking about this in pain, and talk about it in joy. I had to speak life. No more bashing. He said deal with you from the inside out. And that is when #WatchMeSoar went from pain to promise. The pain was still there, but I pushed past my pain and was obedient. I had no idea what my obedience would yield. I started to post positive things and before you knew it, private messages started pouring in. People were hurting and wanted help with getting through it.

Me: How exactly do you help others through their situations?
Chonte': I mentor and coach people who have issues with low self-esteem, who're hurt, heartbroken, angry, and need help with learning ways to deal with their anger. My pain resulted in me walking into my

CHONTE' NICHOL - FROM PAIN TO PROMISE CONT'D

promise. My organization WatchMeSoar Inc. was born out of my pain. SOAR stands for Survive, Obtain, Accomplish, and Reach. You must Survive the pain, to Obtain the promise, to Accomplish your goals, to Reach your destiny.

Me: What does WatchMeSoar offer?
Chonte': WatchMeSoar Inc. offers coaching and mentoring sessions. This year we will start classes and planning has already begun for the first WatchMeSoar conference. This year we're having our 2nd Annual Soar the Runway fashion show. During the model open call for Soar the Runway, we use the casting call to encourage, enhance, and never give negative feedback. With so many others are bringing people down, we make sure we use every given opportunity to lift people up.

Me: Tell me more about Soar the Runway.
Chonte': Soar the Runway Fashion Show was created in honor of my grandmother Anna Hoke. She is still alive; however, she suffers from Alzheimer's. She and my mother Cheryl Hoke have always been profound influences on me as fashionistas. They taught me how to dress and how to be a lady and we use Soar the Runway to pass that on. Last year, we were able to donate some of the proceeds to the American Diabetes Association. This year, our goal is to double last year's donation to the Multiple Sclerosis organization, MS Chapter of Michigan. We are excited to share that we have over 100 models this year in a two-part dynamic show. A children's fashion show later followed by an adult show.

Me: During the planning process, were there setbacks along the way?
Chonte': Oh yes. Can I say heartbroken? During the process I was broken, but the setbacks made me better. I realized that the reward was greater than the pain. There were some things that didn't go to plan, now Victoria Secrets will be in my show. Again, the reward is greater than the pain.

Me: Whatever Whatever came of the relationship between your ex, which yielded the pain? If you don't mind me asking?
Chonte': My ex-husband and I are great. We co-parent are children with no problems. I only speak highly of him and will continue to do.
For everyone out there going through life altering pain. Let that pain be the catalyst you need to catapult you to your promise and SOAR.

Chonte' Nichol is a mother, entrepreneur, singer, song writer, and producer. She is the CEO and founder of Watch Me Soar Inc, a Mentoring Program. You can stay connected via Instagram @chonte_nichol and www.watchmesoarinc.com.

LISA LEWIS ELLIS - A HEART TO SERVE CONT'D

MizCEO: What's next for Lisa personally?
Lisa: Next is enjoying my second chance at love and marriage with my husband Albert T. Ellis. Aside from making memories with him; I'm looking forward to our adult children receiving their spouses and having children for me to love on and spoil to the bone. Laughing hysterically out loud at that thought. God is good to me!

MizCEO: How do you handle setbacks?
Lisa: I've had enough setbacks for a lifetime. #Truth Because my spiritual practice, faith is central to how I exist in the world I default to the that. I cry when I need too. I scream, holler and vent in my prayer time. I seek to learn the lessons so I can move on quickly and rebound from the setback. I've learned at this stage of my life that there is a lesson in everything. There is something to learn about myself.

MizCEO: What is the greatest lesson that you have learned in business?
Lisa: The greatest lesson that I have learned is business is to be myself. Although I continue to attend conferences, masterminds, and various other types of training, I have to be me. I have to do what feels organic to who I am and what I believe. I have learned to chew the meat and spit out the bones as the old folks used to say. What's for me I keep and what isn't I disregard.

MizCEO: What advice would you give to that person who's business is not going great?
Lisa: My advice to that person whose business is not going great and wants to give up is to remember why you are doing business. If it's only to make money then you should give up. However, if the calling to do business to serve and help others then giving up may leave a person abandoned and helpless. When you think about who may be giving up, who may be throwing in the towel on life, who may be stuck and unable to move forward because you want to selfishly withhold your gift/service...don't give up. I've learned that I as I serve commission comes; in that order.

MizCEO: What does it take to have a successful business?
Lisa: Knowing your Self; who are you and what do you bring to the table/marketplace. Sharing your Story; if it's holding you back revise your narrative as needed to serve you as you serve others. Manifesting your S.H.I.N.E.; show up, honestly, intentionally, no, excuses. Faith. Faith to know your purpose and making it your life work to accomplish it!

CHELSEA (STALLING) WHITTINGTON

ALL ABOUT CHELSEA

Introduce yourself and profession to our readers:
My name is Chelsea Lynn Whittington often known as "C WHITT." I am a public relations professional with a career that spans 25 years. I have worked in corporate, governmental, educational and non-profit environments pushing brands and building reputations.
I started my PR consulting firm C WHITT in the fall of 2015. Since then I have amassed a portfolio of nearly 20 clients providing a plethora of services including media relations, interview coaching, social media strategy, event planning, professional writing and voiceovers. I also facilitate workshops around social media etiquette and cyberbullying.

My niche market is growing the brands of small businesses. I want to see them win, so I grind right alongside them as I continue to grow my business as well. I have also been teaching at the collegiate level for the past 17 years. Currently, I am an adjunct professor at Indiana University Northwest in Gary, Indiana where I instruct senior citizens on social media, smartphones, email and internet use. I am also an adjunct professor at Indiana Wesleyan University where I teach communications courses on both undergraduate and graduate levels.

By day, I serve as the Director of External Affairs and Special Events at the Chicago Urban League. I have been married for 9 years to my wonderful husband Terrell, who is my greatest supporter and inspiration!

What inspired you to pursue this area of interest?
The field of public relations actually chose me. After obtaining my first degree in Broadcast Journalism from Howard University, I'd planned to be a talk show host, but every opportunity that crossed my path seemed to be in PR. I earned my Master's Degree in Organizational Communication from Purdue University, and I have been working in the field ever since.

What advice would you share with those interested in a similar pursuit?
Anyone who wants to pursue a career in PR must not have a shy bone in his or her body! Be ready to work longer hours than everyone, and be prepared for all of the attention (good and bad) that come with this profession. Protect your brand at all times, and always make time to reach back and help someone else!

Discuss a professional challenge and how you overcame it:
Several years ago, I found myself involved in a situation where my reputation took a hit. While I was innocent of the accusations, it didn't stop a vast amount of seen and unseen "haters" from attempting to destroy my name. I overcame this professional challenge by looking up, and I don't just mean holding my head up, but looking to God for comfort, strength and direction.

My husband and family were also by my side through the entire ordeal. Looking back, it was probably one of the best things that could have happened to me. Not only did the situation drive me to start my own

CHELSEA (STALLING) WHITTINGTON CONT'D

business, but it gave me the drive to build my brand and bank account to a level that I had never previously imagined! My God is awesome!

What is next for your brand/business in 2018?
Having recently landed a major account, I have now set my sights on expanding my business with a website (didn't need one at first with so many word-of-mouth connections) and perhaps hiring a part-time assistant/writer to help with a few projects. I also plan to book more speaking engagements and facilitate more workshops.

How can readers connect with you online and through social media?
I am on Facebook as Chelsea Stalling Whittington, and my professional page is @CWHITTPR. I am also on LinkedIn, Twitter (clwhittington) and Instagram (clwhittington) I am on Facebook as Chelsea Stalling Whittington, and my professional page is @CWHITTPR. I am also on LinkedIn, Twitter (clwhittington) and Instagram (clwhittington)

What's one thing you know for sure?

JILL AND JOKIMA - THE LITERARY LIFE

Jill & Jokima

Why drives your passion when writing?

Writing is a creative outlet that helps me express my experiences in hospitality after I've had time to process them. I am an avid reader and have always dreamed of seeing my own book in print one day. - Jill

When I look back over my work life, while I haven't experienced everything, I certainly have experienced a lot. I have some crazy stories and if I can help one industry colleague or student better navigate within the industry, then I feel that I must share my stories. - Jokima

What is your best tip for marking your new book?

Initially, we were driven to write because of the day-to-day challenging experiences we experienced together in working in the hotel industry. Now, we draw on our individual, previous and current experiences as industry professionals, educators, and hotel customers. — Jill & Jokima

Tell us about your businesses - how many books have you published?

Our over-arching goal is to educate. We have one book we wrote together entitled "The RevPAR Formula". It is a very helpful guide for anyone interested in getting into the hotel industry. It can also serve as a refresher for seasoned industry veterans.

Our second book entitled "The Red Book" is set to be released this year and is an uncensored account of a new hotel general manager's journey. It is a pretty wild journey! Jokima has a book entitled *"7 EASY Ways to Show Your Employees YOU Care!"* that serves as her love letter to those who manage others. It is another helpful guide for anyone struggling to connect with and engage their employees.

We are also available to serve as guest speakers for students and industry professionals. — Jill & Jokima

What is the difference between professional publishing and self-publishing?

Professional publishing is where a publishing company contracts with you, advances you royalties, and has some weight in what you produce while self-

publishing, you pay for all of the expenses, but what you produce is solely your product. – Jill & Jokima

How do you handle writer's block?
I walk away and read a book of someone else's. I read a favorite novel from an author that I respect and inspires me to get pass the block. – Jill

I have to be in a "writing mode" to begin with which requires a comfortable setting like my kitchen table, comfortable clothing like my pajamas, and something to snack on! - Jokima

What is the greatest lesson that you have learned in business?
We learned that you have to be your biggest fan as no one else will understand your vision as you do! Early on when our book was first published we were so excited and thought all of our family, friends, and industry colleagues would eagerly purchase a copy as well as provide a review of our book. We learned the hard way. – Jill & Jokima

What advice would you give to that person who is struggling in writing their book and wants to give up?
Walking away temporarily to get perspective is ok, but be sure to return with a renewed energy to look at it again. – Jill

Think about your why, in other words think on what pushed you to have your original thought of writing your book. Oftentimes I say, that if it had not been for the dreams of a little girl (me), I would have quit a long time ago. I think of that little girl all the time! - Jokima

In your opinion, what does it take to have a best seller?
Longevity. It may take a lifetime for some authors to be recognized and to reap the benefits of their efforts. So, our goal is to not to get weary in our good doing. We must be persistent. – Jill & Jokima

HEALTH AND WELLNESS - RAVEN LITTLE AND LISA GRAY

By Santisha Walker

A woman desiring to achieve a momentous task will need to possess a great deal of determination. A woman in business with a vision going against the norm in her industry will require even greater staying power! After learning what business owners and nurses, Raven Little and Lisa Gray, and their company, One Drop Health & Wellness, is offering the Charlotte, North Carolina community, I knew these ladies have what it takes to make a profound impact on the lives of others! If you ask Raven and Lisa the overall goal of their business, they will inform you they are, "2 nurses healing the world one drop at a time". Their unconventional start up story and early challenges will encourage any female entrepreneur to stay the course and persevere.

From the moment One Drop Health & Wellness became a thought to officially opening your company's doors, how long did it take you to bring it into fruition?
Lisa - Exactly 1 month. From preparation to it fixing up, then to painting and decorating, the grand opening was exactly one month.

Did you all already have resources in place and assistance before proceeding with the vision?
Raven - No. We just stepped out there. I had this idea and approached Lisa about it. She was very interested, so we decided to move forward. We worked together and made it happen. We're still working on the marketing and in the process of learning how to use technology to reach our target audience. We hired a business coach to help as well; but overall, we simply went for it! What has helped you get to this point in starting and operating your business?
Lisa – The support of our spouse and family has played a major role. Starting a business takes a tremendous amount of work for sure.
Raven – I agree with Lisa. Our husbands have been very supportive. Also, Lisa and my personality really meshed well together. We are opposite in many ways, so it helps cover various areas of the business. Lisa is creative, and I have previous experience with business ownership. We are also flexible with one another and mature enough to get along well with each other.

Let's talk about female competition, which a lot of women deal with. How do you handle competition

HEALTH AND WELLNESS - CONT'D

amongst other women business owners?
Lisa – Society puts a lot of emphasis on competition. I feel women need to come together as a community and network. We can grow just as much when we learn to network with other women.

Raven – We do not believe in female competition. It really doesn't fit us! Lisa and I both believe that there is enough out here for everybody! We just don't think in those terms. We think unlimited. Everything we do, we aim to put that message out to other business owners. We love networking with other businesses, especially minority-owned businesses. We have gone into the community to build relationships with other female entrepreneurs in the area, such as salons and yoga studios. We introduce ourselves and welcome the opportunity to partner and build a bond to enhance the well-being of others.

As business owners, what would you say is your daily struggle?
Lisa – I would say my everyday struggle is balance. Because I still work full-time as a nurse and have a family desiring their time and attention, I'm still learning how to balance owning a business and managing my personal life.

Raven – I agree. I have four children and Lisa has five, so it's difficult with balancing our full- time jobs, business and families. I try to make as much time for my husband and children as I can. Also, I would say another struggle is remaining in tuned with social media and remaining up-to- date with technology to reach others. We have a lot of great free services we offer our community. It's a matter of reaching them to par take in the services we have to offer. We are still learning as we go.

What are your thoughts on the connection between stress and health issues? What are ways to relieve stress?
Lisa – There's a direct correlation between health and stress. Stress is very detrimental to your health. I think it's very important to learn ways to cope and de-stress. If not, you will experience the toll it takes on your health. That brings us back to teaching the community ways to de-stress. Even if it's simply using a diffuser with a relaxing oil blend, there are simple and practical ways to de-stress.

Raven – What I discovered while working in the hospital is that our mental stability is often overlooked. Our physical, mental, emotional well-being and environment all work together and play a major role in our total health. Stress affects every part of your health! One way women can relieve stress is through our company's Vaginal Steam Service. Most women feel they don't have a problem in this area, but it addresses total health. It brings wellness to your digestive system, helps with depression, and promotes better sleep. It also helps heal from sexual trauma and soul ties. It's relaxing and allow women to embrace themselves and have better quality of life. Another way to relieve stress is through Aromatouch Therapy, which utilizes essential oils to help balance your immunity and release stress. You can also use positive affirmations to redirect your mental wellness.

We understand that business ownership is very stressful. During our start-up process, and even now, we make sure we take breaks and return to challenging tasks the next day, as needed. We definitely use our own services. When discouragement comes, I have to tap into my own coping strategies and regroup.

Do you have any upcoming projects, classes, or services?
Raven – Yes. We offer free wellness classes nightly at 6pm Tuesday through Thursday. These classes are centered around topics such as aromatherapy, essential oils, stress, sleep, autism, etc., and how you can utilize various holistic therapies to assist with health concerns. Events and other services are listed on our website and Facebook page.

How can we connect with you?
You can visit our website at onedrop2nurses.com. Also, we are on Facebook and Instagram under @onedrop2nurses. You can visit our location at 1008 Union Road, Suite B Gastonia, NC 28054.

About the Author:
Santisha Walker is a Registered Nurse, Certified Wellness Coach, Entrepreneur, Author, Speaker, and Nurse Branding Coach. She has an immense passion of empowering others to live their best life through total wellness and balanced living. She is a devoted wife to her loving and supportive husband, and appreciations spending time with those she holds dear to her heart. You can connect with Santisha through her boutique consulting company, Walker Group Health & Wellness at walkergrouphw.com, through her personal site at SantishaWalker.com, or through her Facebook and Instagram pages @santishawalkerrn.

LASALLE JACKSON - PURSUING THE DREAM

By Dwan Bryant

When you row, row your boat gently down the stream, according to Lasalle Jackson, life is not always what you dream. With determination and perseverance, you can design the destiny that appears to be impossible but a reality with the right amount of courage.

Dwan: You are such a busy woman! Not only are you a full time college professor, a full time business owner of Affirmatrace, but also a mother and wife. How does this work for you when you have to get specific tasks accomplished in a limited amount of time?
Lasalle: I pray, pray and pray.... I find myself looking up to God because I believe he hears my prayers when my life gets congested. I ask God what does He want me to do with the task ahead of me. What are the next steps, my mission in getting it accomplished without feeling overwhelmed and defeated.

Dwan: When we talk about perseverance, how do you define it as a mother, as a wife, and business owner?
Lasalle: That question is a challenge within itself (laugh). We, as women, persevere through other challenges in our lives that qualify us as survivors. You are molded into a mother and a wife with some situations that you persevere through from your childhood. You have to use those experiences and make the best of it for your own family without creating nasty scars. It was difficult for me at times because I was adopted, and I learned to be a self-starter asking for minimal help. It worked temporarily until I learned I could not do it all on my own. So as a business owner, I soon learned that I could not work every facet of my life by myself.

Dwan: As women, we find ourselves trying to wear every hat even when it doesn't fit. We get prideful and won't ask for help to press through even when we know we need it. How do you push through that phase of your life?
Lasalle: Yes, it's definitely a growing pain with me because I'm used to running things on my own and getting help here and there. But that's life, you have to persist and keep it moving. You have to push yourself out of the dumps and not resort to "poor me" and feeling sorry for yourself because you have the key to control how the wheel will turn. You cannot depend solely on yourself, you must ask for help and learn how to trust others even if you have experienced betrayal in your life.

Dwan: You are absolutely right about learning to trust others, especially other women. But what about trusting yourself and what does that look like for you?
Lasalle: You know, persevering in just trusting yourself is so relevant today in women entrepreneurs. I remember just puddling around with the idea of starting my own business in 2011 but life took a different turn when I was laid off and I was forced to revisit what I initially started. I had to trust that Lasalle had enough in her to launch and make this business work. It's a different type of beast when it actually works, and you have to wrap your mind around the growth and who you will put in place to keep it moving on an upward spiral.

Dwan: I have thoroughly enjoyed your words of wisdom during this interview. What would you say to women who stop and start and have not found the courage to persevere on their journey to go all the way to the top?
Lasalle: Go back to your vision board or that piece of paper where you wrote your plans on. You have to return back to your core values and beliefs and make sure it lines up with the will of God for your life. Stay in tune to what God wants you to do. The truth is

NECOYA TYSON - PLANNING WITH PURPOSE

Planning with purpose

NECOYA TYSON; THE EVENT PLANNER YOU NEED TO KNOW

MizCEO: How long have you been in business?
Nagoya: I've owned my business for 9 years. I'm looking forward to 2019 so that I can celebrate my company's 10 year anniversary with a bang!

MizCEO: Why did you pick this particular field to do business in?
Necoya: It's funny….I actually didn't pick this field to be in. I believe that it chose me. My degree is in Mass Communications (broadcast journalism & production). My entire life I wanted to be a television news anchor; until I found out in college that I truly enjoyed working behind the scenes more. My first job out of college was as a community development coordinator for a non-profit organization where I wrote press releases/media advisories and had the privilege of participating in various speaking engagements. Then I was tasked with planning the company's 10 year anniversary celebration and I've been planning ever since!

Tell us about a challenge you have had in business and how you have overcome it?
The hardest thing for me has been finding the right people for my team that have a work ethic that's inline with mine, my vision and my business goals. To overcome this, I've been working with my mentor and my business coach and started taking management classes. This has truly helped me in figuring out what questions to ask when interviewing, finding out how people deal with adversity in particular situations, and other pertinent things to ask when finding people to work with/for you, especially in the events industry.

MizCEO: Why do you feel you have been as successful as you have in your business?
Necoya: I think that my ability to relate to people

NECOYA TYSON - PLANNING WITH PURPOSE

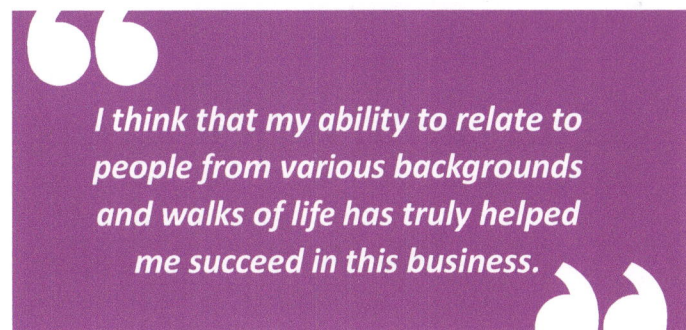

I think that my ability to relate to people from various backgrounds and walks of life has truly helped me succeed in this business.

from various backgrounds and walks of life has truly helped me succeed in this business. I've been in this business for a long time and I've seen a lot. I always put myself in my clients' shoes and try to actually think like them.

MizCEO: Why are you so compelled on seeing other women win BIG?
Necoya: I want to break the stereotype that women to support and push each other to be greater. If I can push and encourage another woman to be greater, better, to follow her dreams and to be a winner, in my eyes that makes us all winners.

MizCEO: So, what's next in 2018 for you?
Nagoya: I launched my wedding workshop series, Mornings are for Mimosas in January of this year. This workshop focuses on budget creation, hiring the right vendors for your wedding day and the importance of having a wedding planner on your big day. Up next will be the second workshop, which will be held in Raleigh, NC in May. It's going to be amazing!

MizCEO: Fun fact about yourself.
Necoya: I am a HUGE Prince fan. HUGE!!! His Purple Highness will go down in history as one of the greatest musicians/performers to ever grace a stage. I'm getting teary-eyed just thinking about him.

MizCEO: How can we stay connected with you?
Necoya: You can find me on Instagram/Twitter/Facebook/Pinterest under @aayouevents or #aayouevents

LASALLE JACKSON - PURSUING THE DREAM CONT'D

in tune to what God wants you to do. The truth is maybe you created an expectation you have not yet grown mentally to meet just yet so rewrite some of your goals based on what you are willing to do in the current stage of your life. God wants you to move forward so He can bless you. It may not be with the millions of dollars right away but He will bless you in a way that you can be a blessing to others.

Lasalle Jackson
Founder/CEO of Affirmatrace
lasallejackson@yahoo.com
http://www.affirmatrace.com/

Dwan Bryant, is an inspirational speaker, Confidence Life Coach, best-selling author and Founder and CEO of Confident Woman on the Move. Dwan's mission is to inspire confidence in women of all cultures globally with a message of affirmation and liberation that grants women permission to unapologetically walk in confidence. Confident Woman, the journey begins right now. One Mind. One Unity. One Mission. Women. Dwan can be reached via Facebook and Twitter as Dwan Bryant and dbryantmotivational.com.

FOR THE ENTREPRENEURIAL WOMAN.

Empowering. Uplifting. Inspirational.

www.ingramcontent.com/pod-product-compliance
Lightning Source LLC
Chambersburg PA
CBHW040450220526
45473CB00004B/1582